IT'S TIME TO EAT BROWNIES

It's Time to Eat BROWNIES

Walter the Educator

Silent King Books
A WhichHead Entertainment Imprint

Copyright © 2025 by Walter the Educator

All rights reserved. No part of this book may be reproduced in any manner whatsoever without written per- mission except in the case of brief quotations embodied in critical articles and reviews.

First Printing, 2024

Disclaimer

This book is a literary work; the story is not about specific persons, locations, situations, and/or circumstances unless mentioned in a historical context. Any resemblance to real persons, locations, situations, and/or circumstances is coincidental. This book is for entertainment and informational purposes only. The author and publisher offer this information without warranties expressed or implied. No matter the grounds, neither the author nor the publisher will be accountable for any losses, injuries, or other damages caused by the reader's use of this book. The use of this book acknowledges an understanding and acceptance of this disclaimer.

It's Time to Eat BROWNIES is a collectible early learning book by Walter the Educator suitable for all ages belonging to Walter the Educator's Time to Eat Book Series. Collect more books at WaltertheEducator.com

USE THE EXTRA SPACE TO TAKE NOTES AND DOCUMENT YOUR MEMORIES

BROWNIES

It's time to eat, oh what a treat!

It's Time to Eat
Brownies

Something chocolatey and sweet.

Soft and chewy, rich and round,

The best dessert that I have found!

Warm and gooey, fresh and thick,

I can't wait to take a lick!

Baked with love and full of cheer,

Brownies bring us joy right here!

Pick one up, it feels so light,

Take a nibble, what a bite!

Fudgy middle, crispy top,

Once I start, I just can't stop!

Some have sprinkles, some have nuts,

Some have caramel in their cuts.

Frosted, plain, or filled with chips,

Every brownie's good to sip!

It's Time to Eat
Brownies

Mom and Dad both take a square,

Sister grabs one from the air!

Brother smiles and says, "Oh wow!

Can I have one more right now?"

Stack them up or eat them slow,

Either way, they taste just so!

Chewy, chocolate, oh so grand,

I love brownies, yes, I do!

Oh no! My plate is empty now,

I want more, but don't know how!

Just one more? I smile and say,

Maybe save some for the day?

Brownie fun is best to share,

With my family everywhere.

Picnics, parties, late at night,

It's Time to Eat
Brownies

Brownies make the world so bright!

Now my tummy's full and tight,

Every bite was such delight!

Chocolate smiles, joy inside,

Brownies fill my heart with pride!

Time for bed, the stars shine bright,

Dreams of brownies through the night.

Tomorrow's snack? Oh yes, indeed,

It's Time to Eat
Brownies

More sweet brownies, what a need!

ABOUT THE CREATOR

Walter the Educator is one of the pseudonyms for Walter Anderson. Formally educated in Chemistry, Business, and Education, he is an educator, an author, a diverse entrepreneur, and he is the son of a disabled war veteran. "Walter the Educator" shares his time between educating and creating. He holds interests and owns several creative projects that entertain, enlighten, enhance, and educate, hoping to inspire and motivate you. Follow, find new works, and stay up to date with Walter the Educator™

at WaltertheEducator.com

www.ingramcontent.com/pod-product-compliance
Lightning Source LLC
LaVergne TN
LVHW010622070526
838199LV00063BA/5242